Praise for

The Leadership Cube

Turning Leadership Complexity into Leadership Clarity

David Theilacker's "The Leadership Cube" provides invaluable examples which will be of great value to those who are charged with attaining goals by marshaling the best from their team.

Michael L. George Sr.

Best Selling Author of Lean Six Sigma, BS, MS Physics, Founder and Chairman of the George Group, and Principle at Blackland Private Equity Group.

The Leadership Cube is an important addition to the body of work addressing organizational effective processes. It specifically addresses goals, responsibilities, and accountabilities for all whom are part of every level of business organizations. David Theilacker has chosen an interesting analogy with the Rubik's cube. When combined with his leadership workshops, it is a powerful practical tool. I would strongly recommend this journey as a way to organizational success, taught by a master of continuous process improvement.

Vice Admiral Walter B. Massenburg, USN (Retired)

Former Commander, Naval Air Systems Command

The Leadership Cube

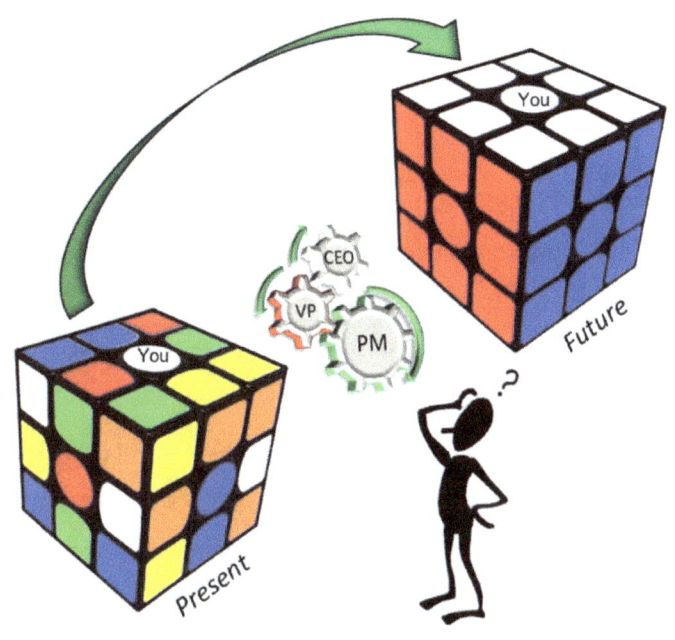

Turning Leadership Complexity into

Leadership Clarity

David J. Theilacker

ISBN: 9798397053211

Imprint: Independently published

Hasbro, Inc. is the exclusive licensee for the Rubik's Cube trademark in the United States.

This book is dedicated to my wife Leslie.

This book is dedicated to you, my wife, my greatest source of inspiration, and my unwavering support in all my endeavors. Your unwavering belief in me has propelled me to new heights and has given me the strength to embrace the challenges that come with leadership.

I am eternally grateful for your presence in my life.

Thank you for being my rock, my cheerleader, and my best friend. Without you, this book and my leadership journey would have been incomplete. Your unwavering support has given me the courage to step into my full potential as a leader.

With all my love and gratitude,

David J. Theilacker

Table of Contents

Introduction

The Rubik's Cube is an excellent visual analogy for the complexity of leadership, where the different layers, sides and colors of the cube visually represent the different components of an organization.

The Rubik's Cube is a complex iconic puzzle that has captured the imagination of millions around the world. While it may seem like a simple toy, it has the potential to be much more. In fact, the Rubik's Cube can be used as a visual tool to turn leadership complexity into leadership clarity.

Assessing the present state of an organization using a Rubik's Cube analogy involves analyzing each side of the cube to identify areas that are not aligned. This can include leadership styles, individuals' motivation and ability. By understanding these factors, organizations can determine where misalignment exists and work towards a more cohesive and effective leadership approach.

Using the Rubik's Cube analogy, it's possible to assess the present state of an organization. This involves looking at the different sides of the cube and evaluating the alignment of the colors.

Just as in a Rubik's Cube, each side color of the cube can represent different components of an organization, such as corporate operations, sales, purchasing and administration. By evaluating the alignment of these components, it's possible to get a clear understanding of the present state of the organization.

Once the present state has been assessed, it's possible to apply learned or existing leadership styles (a mix if needed) and individual motivation/ability initiatives to the future state of the organization.

This involves understanding the different leadership styles, such as Autocratic Leadership Style, Democratic Leadership Style, Servant Leadership Style and Transformational Leadership Style, and how they can be applied to achieve the organization's goals. It also involves understanding the motivations and abilities of the individual in the organization and aligning them with the organization's vision.

Applying continuous improvements to the future state of an organization is critical for long-term success.[1] Leaders must work together to establish a shared vision and strategy that aligns with the organization's goals. Senior Leadership (middle managers) must translate this vision into actionable plans, and Individual Contributors must understand their roles and responsibilities to effectively execute these plans.

By using the Rubik's Cube as a visual tool, organizations can achieve leadership clarity and create a culture of alignment, teamwork, and success.

This book is a "Practical Nonfiction" book. Meaning it presents information, advice, or guidance on a specific topic in a straightforward, clear, and accessible manner.

This book is aimed to help readers solve a problem or acquire new skills, knowledge, or insights related to real-life situations and is based on the author's expertise, research, or personal experiences, and provide readers with actionable advice. It is designed to inform, educate, and empower readers to achieve their goals and improve their lives.

Endnotes

1. George, Michael L. Sr, Dan Blackwell, and Michael L. George Jr. 2019. Lean Six Sigma in the Age of Artificial Intelligence: Harnessing the Power of the Fourth Industrial Revolution. New York: McGraw-Hill Education.

Chapter One: The Analogy

Rubik's Cube, the iconic 3D puzzle, has been entertaining and challenging people for decades. Over the years, people have developed and refined algorithms to solve the Rubik's Cube efficiently.

Interestingly, these algorithms can be used as a metaphor for solving some of the most complex issues facing leadership of an organization today.

In this chapter, we will explore how the Rubik's Cube can be used as a visual tool to turn leadership complexity into leadership clarity and is especially useful to the visual learner.

Who are you?

You may be the Owner, Chief Executive Officer (CEO) or President of your organization, represented by the "center logo" on a Rubik's Cube.

You may be Executive Leadership represented by the first layer of a Rubik's Cube.

You may be Senior Leadership, or an Individual Contributor represented respectfully by the second and third layer of a Rubik's Cube.

Do you have a clear well-defined leadership strategy that is in alignment with your organization's North Star?

Leaders are located at every layer of an organization. It is your responsibility, as a leader, to ensure that you and your team fully understand your organization's alignment strategies.

Everyone in your organization should understand your organization's goals, what their responsibilities are in achieving them and what the goals are to each other.

The objective of this chapter is to visually give you a better understanding of what leadership alignment looks like and why it is paramount that everyone in your organization recognizes that their work is critical to the organization in reaching its goals.

It also helps you to visualize all the complex parts of an organization working together towards a common purpose. It gives you a better understanding of alignment/accountability and how everyone's roles are so important and gives you a better understanding of how leadership alignment processes begin.

For example, beginning with Executive Leadership establishing clear long-term alignment goals and objectives. In addition, these objectives, at minimum, may assist you with a leadership style that feels authentic to you (maybe a mix of styles) and help bring out the leadership potential that is already within you.

Understanding the Layers of the Cube

Imagine a Rubik's Cube, with its nine squares on each side, representing the different members of a team. Just like the colors on a Rubik's Cube, each member brings a unique set of skills, strengths, and perspectives to the team.

Each layer of the Rubik's Cube can also represent different layers of responsibilities. For example, the Top Layer/Executive Leadership, Middle Layer/Senior Leadership, Bottom Layer/Individual Contributors (depending on how your organization is organized).

The sides of the cube can represent four product lines (i.e., Green Side/Sales, Red Side/Purchasing, Orange Side/Administration, Blue Side/Operations).

Seeing your organization from a different perspective. Turning leadership complexity into leadership clarity:

"A scrambled cube represents the misaligned state of an organization."

- First Layer represents Executive Leadership (i.e. You, Owner, President, Vice Presidents, Directors, Trusted Advisors).

- Second Layer represents Senior Leadership (i.e. You, Product-Line Managers, Team Leads).

- Third Layer represents Individual Contributors (individuals with limited managerial organizational responsibilities).

Setting Clear Alignment Strategies

Setting clear alignment strategies for each of your individuals is the beginning foundation leading to significant "Common Sense" improvements.

The alignment goals, objectives, and expected outcomes for executives, managers, and individual contributors are all aligned with the mission of the organization, creating a common understanding of expectations throughout the organization.

Effective alignment strategies create an ideal environment for high-performing teams to become enthusiastic leaders or participants in current and future improvement initiatives.

These initiatives are designed to achieve maximum impact with minimal effort, ultimately driving the organization closer to its goals.

By employing clear alignment strategies, individuals are inspired to gain a deeper comprehension of how their work directly contributes to the overarching goals of the company.

Five ways to set your people up for success:

1. Leadership needs to be on the same page.

2. Set clear goals for each individual employee.

3. Connect the dots with your individuals and product lines goals with Leadership goals (Rubik's Cube analogy).

4. Structure all work properly (some will be very achievable; some will be more of a stretch).

5. Properly diagnose employee development level (i.e., using Blanchard's SLII® model).[2]

These direct linkages also create a cascading process that fosters enhanced communication, increased employee engagement, and more efficient and effective operations. Clear alignment strategies can create performance expectations and establish accountability.

Chapter Summary/Key Takeaways

The leadership alignment process is remarkably like solving a Rubik's Cube. There are numerous possible combinations to solve a Rubik's Cube (43 quintillion possible combinations). In business, there are also numerous combinations that can be deployed to strategically align an organization.

Using a Top/Down approach, our focus on aligning an organization is analogous to solving a Rubik's Cube (one layer at a time). In the following chapters, we will look at the different stages of solving the Rubik's Cube top layer, continuing down to the middle layer and then the bottom layer (Beginner's Method).

Each layer of the Rubik's Cube represents different layers of responsibilities/accountability (depending on how you're organized).

Known algorithms used in solving layers two and three, represent "Best Business Practices." These best business practices can be replicated in other areas of your organization (or business units) as process improvement initiatives (i.e., your hiring process, your training process).

Endnotes

2. Ridge, Garry, and Ken Blanchard. 2009. Helping People Win at Work: A Business Philosophy Called "Don't Mark My Paper, Help Me Get an A" 1st ed. Pearson.

Chapter Two: Assessing the Present State

You are the center (logo) of your organization. Do you have clear well defined "goals" aligning your organization to your "North Star"?

It is your responsibility to ensure everyone in your organization understands your goals.

When using the Rubik's Cube analogy, which cube best represents the present state of your organization?

Seeing the need for alignment should be obvious. If it is and your organization resembles that of a solved cube, congratulations your organization is in full alignment. If not and your organization resembles more of a scrambled cube, your organization is not in full alignment.

However, because you recognize that your organization is not in full alignment, you completed the first step towards alignment (recognizing a need for change). Sometimes it's not so obvious. So, what's next?

A scrambled cube represents the misaligned state of an organization. Seeing the need for alignment is critical and/or there may be a need to set clear goals for all individuals.

Executive Leadership Aligning to the Organizations Goals

The first layer of a Rubik's Cube represents Executive Leadership (i.e., You, Owner, President, Vice Presidents, Directors, Trusted Advisors).

Your role entails establishing explicit objectives and formulating performance expectations that will lay the groundwork for future conversations on progress, autonomy, and resource requirements.

This foundation is essential for building and sustaining a strategically aligned organization.

As an Executive Leader, your focus on strategy can help ensure the success of your organization's mission. Asking yourself a few useful strategic assessment questions may help you develop an effective plan of action for both short-term and long-term goals.

- Has the organization established an integration process that creates a governance process that includes all key stakeholders?

- Do all members of the Executive Leadership Team (the first layer of the Rubik's Cube) possess knowledge of the priorities required to implement and accelerate strategic alignment throughout all layers of your organization?

- Do you have a business plan that is aligned with the organization's mission and strategic direction?

- What is your organization's strategic direction for the short-term (1-3 years) and long-term (4-5 years)?

- What are your top organizational strengths and challenges?

- How well-positioned is your organization to survive change (e.g., increase/loss of partners, budget, programs, etc.)?

- Have metrics been established that will assess whether or not your organization is meeting its cost, schedule and performance objectives?

- Have you conducted a workforce analysis based on what you see (i.e., any functions that could potentially be consolidated, including any skills or positions that could be outsourced)?

Senior Leadership Aligning to Organizations Alignment Goals

The second layer of the Rubik's Cube represents Senior Leadership (i.e. You, Middle Managers, Product Line Team Leads).

Become more aware of your goal-setting habits. Have you optimized the challenge inherent in each person's goals or tasks, or have you fallen into the habit of overusing and under-challenging your best people?

Many organizations develop lazy goal setting habits that don't really challenge their best people.

- Do you establish and foster cross agency collaboration to achieve common goals and objectives?

- Do you ensure that your staff partners across functional areas leverage program experiences and expertise to resolve challenging issues (i.e., all levels of the Rubik's Cube)?

- Do you capture lessons learned and outcomes of these collaborative efforts and ensure they are collected, and shared across the organization as a way to showcase and strengthen the collaborative process?

- Do you continuously partner with stakeholders in your organization to capture input and suggestions on leadership goals, measures, and impact?

- Do you ensure strategic, operational, and employee measures are aligned with the mission and goals of the organization, specific programs, and individual organizations?

- Do you lead continuous process improvement assessments on multiple levels of the organization? Continuous process improvement assessments provide the foundation for communicating and improving organization related outcomes.

Individual Contributors Critical to an Organizations Alignment Goals

The third layer represents Individual Contributors (individuals with limited organizational managerial responsibilities).

Everyone needs to know that their work is meaningful with clear alignment between what they do and what the organization is trying to accomplish.

Have you interviewed and more importantly "listened" to the Individual Contributors within your organization?

If you can't point to a key objective and how an individual contributor's work is impacting it, you do not have a strategically aligned organization. You may want to build or to evaluate your performance management system.

Building a performance culture goes far beyond an agency's performance management system.

- The performance management system provides a framework for setting objectives, documenting performance standards, and assessing employee results.

- A performance culture refers to the agency's holistic approach to performance (i.e., ongoing, timely feedback; emphasis on continuous learning; strong employee engagement; inclusion and appreciation of a diverse workforce; and accountability for results).

- Timely feedback and continuous learning provide a mechanism for ongoing improvement.

- Work-Life programs support the employee thereby enhancing productivity, engagement with the agency, and sense of well-being.

In addition to seeking out and attracting motivated and skilled individuals to fulfill current requirements, you must also consider how you will help your organization live up to future ones.

Effective leadership alignment planning is essential in an organization. However, those systems cannot stand on their own. You play a critical role in your organization's success. The next step in determining how to cultivate a work environment that supports and sustains a culture of superior performance is needed to drive success both in the organization's present state and future state.

Chapter Summary/Key Takeaways

You are the center of your company. You have clear-defined leadership alignment goals. Everyone in your company understands your goals and understands how their work contributes to your goals.

Everyone needs to know that their work is meaningful with clear alignment between what they do and what the organization is trying to accomplish. If you can't point to a key departmental objective and how an employee's work is impacting it, you do not have the alignment that your organization needs.

Properly diagnosed development levels are critical for tasks requiring an employee to be self-sufficient or to establish where autonomy is deserved and should be established.

For tasks that are beyond an employee's current skill level and immediate resources, an agreement for direction and support is needed. Determining an employee's development level is a key leadership attribute.

Chapter Three: Leadership Style Considerations

Recognizing that there are numerous leadership styles, consider the leadership style that feels authentic to you (it may be a mix of styles).

Look at bringing out the leadership potential that is already within you, recognizing the need to continuously tune-up your perspective on how you lead within your work, family, and friends.

Leadership is an essential aspect of any organization, and the style of leadership used can significantly impact the success of *the organization.*

"Always remember, management is about an individual's position, leadership is about you as an individual."

Do you recognize any of the leadership styles represented in the following illustrations?

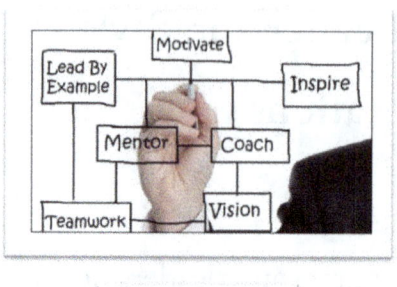

How are you seen by your peers?

Effective leadership is not only about the individual's personal traits but also about their leadership style.

A leader's style of leadership is influenced by various factors such as organizational culture, team dynamics, and individual preferences. The following are some of the leadership style considerations that can impact a leader's success in their role.

Authoritarian Leadership Style

Authoritarian leadership style, also known as autocratic leadership, is a leadership style where the leader makes all the decisions and exercises a high level of control over the team. This style of leadership is characterized by a hierarchical structure with a clear chain of command, where the leader dictates what needs to be done, how it should be done, and when it should be done.

The authoritarian leader expects their team members to follow their orders without questioning them, and they may enforce strict rules and regulations to ensure compliance.[3]

The authoritarian leadership style can be effective in certain situations, such as during a crisis or emergency, where quick decisions need to be made to prevent further damage. In such situations, the leader's ability to make quick, decisive decisions can be critical to the success of the team.

Additionally, when team members lack the necessary skills or experience to make independent decisions, the authoritarian leadership style can be beneficial because it provides them with clear guidance and direction.

However, the authoritarian leadership style can also have negative consequences. The strict hierarchy and lack of autonomy can lead to a lack of creativity and innovation in the team, resulting in demotivated individuals.

Team members may feel undervalued and unappreciated, and they may not feel empowered to contribute their ideas and suggestions. Additionally, the authoritarian leadership style can lead to an unhealthy power dynamic, where the leader's authority is unquestioned, and team members may feel afraid to speak up or express their opinions.

In summary, while the authoritarian leadership style can be effective in certain situations, it may not be the best approach for every team or organization. Leaders should consider their team members' skills and experience, as well as the specific circumstances of the situation, before deciding on the appropriate leadership style.

Additionally, leaders should strive to create a positive and empowering work environment that encourages creativity, innovation, and open communication, regardless of the leadership style they choose.

Democratic Leadership Style

The Democratic Leadership Style, also known as participative leadership, is a leadership approach that emphasizes collaboration and inclusiveness in decision-making. In this style of leadership, the leader actively seeks and values the input and opinions of their team members, encourages open communication, and involves the team in the decision-making process.

The leader in a democratic leadership style acts more as a facilitator than a directive authority figure, creating an environment that allows the team to be involved in the decision-making process, and leveraging their knowledge, skills, and experience.

The leader also encourages team members to express their opinions and ideas, listens to their feedback, and considers their input before making a final decision.

The democratic leadership style is effective in situations where the team members have the necessary skills and experience to make independent decisions. This style of leadership fosters a sense of ownership and accountability among team members, leading to increased motivation and job satisfaction.

When team members feel that they are part of the decision-making process, they are more likely to be committed to the organization's goals and feel more invested in the success of the team.

Additionally, the democratic leadership style promotes creativity and innovation. By allowing team members to share their ideas and participate in decision-making, the leader creates an environment where different perspectives and ideas can be discussed, leading to more creative and innovative solutions.

This style also helps to develop the team's problem-solving skills, as team members are encouraged to take initiative and find solutions to challenges.

Overall, the democratic leadership style can be an effective approach for leaders who want to foster collaboration, creativity, and accountability among their team members.

By involving the team in decision-making and valuing their input, leaders can create a more engaged and motivated workforce, leading to better outcomes for the organization.

Servant Leadership Style

Servant Leadership is a style of leadership that prioritizes the needs and well-being of the team members over the goals and objectives of the organization. In this style of leadership, the leader assumes the role of a servant to the team and works to provide them with the support, guidance, and resources they need to achieve their goals.

This leadership style is effective in situations where the team members require a high level of support, and the focus is on their development and growth.

The Servant Leadership Style was first coined by Robert K. Greenleaf in 1970.[4] According to Greenleaf, a servant leader is someone who puts the needs of others first and helps them develop and perform at their best. Servant leaders are not only concerned with achieving results but also with the personal and professional growth of their team members.

Whenever we have an opportunity or responsibility to influence the thinking and the behavior of others, the first choice we are called to make is whether to see the moment through the eyes of self-interest or for the benefit of those we are leading.[5]

In a Servant Leadership environment, the leader works to create a culture of trust and collaboration, where team members feel valued and supported. They foster an environment of open communication, active listening, and empathy, which helps them understand the needs and concerns of their team members.

Servant leaders are also adept at identifying and leveraging the strengths of their team members. They help team members identify their strengths, skills, and talents and use them to achieve their goals. They provide regular feedback, coaching, and mentoring to help team members develop their skills and reach their full potential.

Furthermore, Servant Leadership involves a strong focus on ethical and moral leadership. Servant leaders prioritize the greater good over their own interests, and they work to create positive change in the world. They are committed to serving the needs of others and contributing to the well-being of society as a whole.

Overall, the Servant Leadership Style is an effective approach for leaders who prioritize the growth and development of their team members.

Transformational Leadership Style

Transformational leadership is a leadership style that emphasizes inspiring and motivating team members to achieve their full potential. This style of leadership is characterized by leaders who have a clear vision, strong communication skills, and a focus on empowering their team members to succeed.

Transformational leaders set high expectations for their team members and provide the necessary support and resources to enable them to achieve their goals.

One of the key aspects of transformational leadership is the emphasis on creating a shared vision for the team. Leaders who practice this style work to ensure that everyone on the team understands the overall goals and objectives, and how their individual contributions fit into the bigger picture. This helps to create a sense of purpose and shared ownership among team members.

Another important characteristic of transformational leadership is the emphasis on developing and empowering team members.

Leaders who practice this style work to identify the strengths and weaknesses of their team members and provide opportunities for growth and development. They also work to create a culture of trust and collaboration, where team members feel empowered to take risks and share their ideas.

Transformational leadership is particularly effective in situations that require a high level of innovation and creativity[6]. By creating a culture of empowerment and collaboration, transformational leaders can unlock the full potential of their team members, leading to new and innovative ideas.

This style of leadership is also effective in situations where there is a need for significant change or transformation, as it helps to create a shared vision and a sense of purpose among team members.

Overall, transformational leadership is a powerful style of leadership that can have a significant impact on the success of a team or organization. By focusing on inspiring and motivating team members to achieve their full potential, transformational leaders can create a culture of innovation and creativity, leading to improved performance and success.

Laissez-Faire Leadership Style

This style of leadership is characterized by a hands-off approach, with the leader providing minimal guidance or direction to the team members.

This style of leadership can be effective in certain situations, especially when team members have a high level of autonomy and are capable of making independent decisions.

The Laissez-Faire leadership style is one of the most hands-off approaches to leadership. This style is characterized by leaders providing minimal guidance or direction to their team members. Instead, they let their team members operate independently and make decisions on their own.

When team members are highly skilled, experienced, and self-motivated, they often require less direction and guidance from their leaders. In these situations, a Laissez-Faire leadership style can help team members feel trusted, respected, and empowered.

They are given the freedom to take ownership of their work, and this can lead to increased motivation, creativity, and innovation. Additionally, this style can help build a sense of camaraderie and mutual trust between the leader and team members.

However, there are also drawbacks to this leadership style. One of the most significant risks associated with Laissez-Faire leadership is a lack of accountability. When leaders are hands-off, team members may not receive enough feedback or direction to ensure that they are meeting expectations. This can lead to complacency, mistakes, and ultimately, demotivated individuals.

Furthermore, without clear direction, team members may struggle to prioritize their work, leading to confusion and inefficiency. In situations where team members are less experienced or less self-motivated, the Laissez-Faire style may result in team members feeling unsupported, leading to a lack of confidence and decreased morale.

Overall, the Laissez-Faire leadership style can be effective in certain situations, but it requires careful consideration of the team members' skills, experience, and motivation levels. To be effective, leaders must strike a balance between providing enough guidance and support while still allowing their team members the freedom to operate independently.

In conclusion, effective leadership is a key driver of organizational success. A leader's style and approach to leading their team are important factors that influence the team's performance, productivity, and overall satisfaction. Therefore, choosing the right leadership style is critical to achieving success.

There are various leadership styles, each with its own set of advantages and disadvantages. The authoritarian leadership style, for example, involves making all decisions alone without consulting team members. This style can be useful in emergency situations where quick decisions are necessary. However, it can also lead to resentment and decreased motivation among team members. On the other hand, the democratic leadership style encourages participation and collaboration among team members.

This style can lead to increased job satisfaction and team morale. However, it can also be time-consuming and may result in slower decision-making.

The servant leadership style emphasizes the leader's responsibility to serve their team and prioritize their needs. This style can lead to increased trust and respect among team members. The transformational leadership style involves inspiring and motivating team members to achieve a common goal. This style can lead to increased innovation and creativity within the team.

Finally, the laissez-faire leadership style involves giving team members a high degree of autonomy and letting them make decisions on their own. This style can be effective with experienced and self-motivated team members but can lead to a lack of direction and accountability.

Ultimately, the success of a leader depends on their ability to choose the right leadership style that aligns with their team's needs, organizational culture, and individual preferences. The right leadership style can result in increased motivation, productivity, and job satisfaction for team members, which in turn, contributes to the success of the organization.

What leadership style do you need to have?

Leadership style plays a pivotal role in shaping the success and performance of an organization. The effectiveness of a leader is closely linked to their ability to understand and meet the unique needs of their team and the organization.

To drive positive outcomes, effective leaders must possess the capacity to adapt their leadership style to suit the circumstances they face.

Every team and organization are distinct, characterized by its own set of goals, culture, and dynamics. A one-size-fits-all approach to leadership is rarely effective in addressing the diverse challenges and aspirations present in today's dynamic work environment. Effective leaders recognize this and embrace the flexibility required to adapt their leadership style to the specific context.

Adapting leadership style involves assessing the situation, understanding the capabilities and motivations of team members, and aligning leadership behaviors accordingly. For instance, a visionary and charismatic leadership style may be suitable when leading a team through a period of significant change or inspiring them to pursue ambitious goals. Conversely, a democratic or participative leadership style might be more effective in fostering collaboration and empowering team members to contribute their insights and ideas.

By adapting their leadership style, effective leaders can foster a positive work environment that promotes trust, engagement, and growth. They can empower their team members to take ownership of their work, encourage innovation and creativity, and provide appropriate support and guidance. Moreover, adaptable leaders can tailor their communication strategies, decision-making approaches, and motivational techniques to match the needs and preferences of their team members.

In summary, the success of an organization hinges on the leadership style employed by its leaders. Adaptable leaders who can flexibly adjust their approach to suit the specific needs of their team and organization are more likely to inspire high performance, cultivate a positive work culture, and achieve organizational goals.

By recognizing the importance of adapting their leadership style, leaders can maximize their impact and drive sustainable success in their organizations.

Here are some "Key" leadership style considerations that leaders should keep in mind when leading their team.

1. Situational Leadership

One of the most important considerations for a leader is the ability to adapt to the situation at hand. Situational leadership is the concept that leaders must adjust their leadership style to the situation they are facing.

This means that leaders must be able to recognize when their team needs more direction and when they need more autonomy. It also means that leaders must be able to recognize the strengths and weaknesses of their team members and adjust their leadership style accordingly.

2. Communication

Effective communication is critical in any leadership role. Leaders must be able to communicate clearly and effectively with their team members. This means that they must be able to listen actively to their team members, provide feedback, and delegate tasks effectively.

Leaders must also be able to communicate their vision for the organization and motivate their team members to work towards that vision.

3. Emotional Intelligence

Emotional intelligence is the ability to recognize and understand one's own emotions and the emotions of others. Effective leaders must have high emotional intelligence so that they can build strong relationships with their team members.

This means that leaders must be able to empathize with their team members, understand their perspectives, and respond appropriately to their emotions.

4. Decision Making

Effective leaders must be able to make decisions quickly and effectively. This means that they must be able to analyze information and make informed decisions based on that analysis. Leaders must also be able to communicate their decisions clearly and provide a rationale for their decisions.

5. Delegation

Delegation is the process of assigning tasks to team members. Effective leaders must be able to delegate tasks effectively so that they can focus on more strategic tasks. This means that leaders must be able to recognize the strengths and weaknesses of their team members and assign tasks accordingly. Leaders must also be able to provide clear instructions and guidelines for completing tasks.

6. Coaching and Development

Effective leaders must be able to coach and develop their team members. This means that leaders must be able to provide feedback on performance, identify areas for improvement, and provide training and development opportunities.

Leaders must also be able to recognize the potential of their team members and provide opportunities for growth and advancement.

In conclusion, leadership style considerations are critical for effective leadership. Leaders must be able to adapt their leadership style to the situation at hand, communicate effectively, have high emotional intelligence, make decisions quickly and effectively, delegate tasks effectively, and coach and develop their team members.

Recognizing that there are numerous leadership styles, consider a leadership style that feels authentic to you (maybe a mix of styles). Look at bringing out the leadership potential that is already within you and your team and recognize the need to tune-up your perspective on how you lead within your work.

Teaming Up for Performance

Imagine a Rubik's Cube, with its nine squares on each side, representing the different members of a team. Just like the colors on a Rubik's Cube, each member brings a unique set of skills, strengths, and perspectives to the team.

The ability to work effectively in a team is an essential skill for success in today's fast-paced and interconnected world[7]. Just like a Rubik's Cube, teamwork requires coordination, collaboration, and a shared vision to achieve the desired outcome.

To achieve high performance, each team member needs to work together in harmony, just like turning the cube's rows and columns to align the colors on each side.

Here are three tips to help you and your team "team up" for success using the Rubik's Cube analogy.

1. Start with a clear goal

The first step to effective teamwork is to start with a clear goal. This means defining what you want to achieve as a team and setting measurable objectives that everyone can work towards. Just like the first layer of a Rubik's Cube, it's essential to have a solid foundation on which to build.

Just as you start solving a Rubik's Cube with the goal of aligning all the layers and colors, your team should have a clear understanding of the end goal.

Define what you want to achieve and break it down into achievable steps. Then, assign roles and responsibilities to each team member to ensure everyone is working towards the same goal.

In order to establish a clear goal, it's important to consider the following questions:

- What are we trying to achieve as a team?

- How will we measure success?

- What are the key milestones we need to hit along the way?

- What are the potential challenges we may face, and how will we overcome them?

By answering these questions together as a team, you can establish a shared understanding of what you want to achieve and how you plan to get there.

2. Communicate effectively

Effective communication is crucial to the success of any team. In the context of a Rubik's Cube, each team member needs to know which rows and columns to turn to align the colors on their side. Similarly, in a team, everyone needs to communicate clearly and transparently to ensure that they are on the same page. Encourage open communication and active listening to avoid misunderstandings and conflicts. Just like the middle layer of a Rubik's Cube, communication is the glue that holds everything together.

To communicate effectively, it's important to:

- Listen actively: Be present and attentive when others are speaking. Try to understand their perspective and ask clarifying questions if needed.

- Speak clearly: Be concise and articulate when conveying your ideas. Avoid using jargon or technical terms that others may not understand.

- Provide feedback: Offer constructive feedback to your teammates when appropriate. Be specific and focus on behaviors or actions rather than personal characteristics.

- Foster open dialogue: Encourage open and honest communication within the team. Create an environment where everyone feels comfortable sharing their thoughts and ideas.

By communicating effectively, you can ensure that everyone is on the same page and working towards the same goal.

3. Leverage each other's strengths

Just like each side of a Rubik's Cube has a different color, each team member has a unique set of skills and strengths. By leveraging each other's strengths, you can achieve high performance as a team.

Assign tasks that align with each member's expertise and encourage everyone to share their ideas and perspectives.

Every team member brings unique skills and strengths to the table. Just like the top layer of a Rubik's Cube, each piece is different and plays a specific role in the overall puzzle.

To leverage each other's strengths, it's important to:

- Identify individual strengths: Take the time to understand each team member's strengths and how they can contribute to the team's success.

- Assign roles and responsibilities: Assign roles and responsibilities based on each team member's strengths and interests.

- Collaborate: Encourage collaboration among team members to leverage each other's strengths and achieve the best possible outcome.

- Support each other: Be supportive of each other and offer help or guidance when needed.

By leveraging each other's strengths, you can create a strong and cohesive team that can tackle any challenge.

Chapter Summary/Key Takeaways

Teaming up for performance is essential for achieving success in today's world. Just like a Rubik's Cube, effective teamwork requires coordination, collaboration, and a shared vision to achieve the desired outcome. Through collaboration, creativity, and communication, individuals can leverage their strengths and skills to accomplish more than any one person could on their own.

By working together towards a common goal, teams can build a sense of camaraderie and mutual support that leads to high performance and success. By starting with a clear goal, communicating effectively, and leveraging each other's strengths, you can create a high-performing team that can overcome any obstacle.

By keeping these considerations in mind, leaders can create a strong and effective team that is capable of achieving their organizational goals.

Endnotes

3. Nilsen, Eric. 2022. The Origins of Authoritarianism - and Why It Still Works Today: From Historical Strongmen and Key Authoritarian Moments in History to Modern ... Today. Independently Published.

4. Greenleaf, Robert K., and Larry C. Spears. 2002. Servant Leadership: A Journey into the Nature of Legitimate Power and Greatness. 25th ed. Paulist Press.

5. Blanchard, Ken, and Phil Hodges. 2003. The Servant Leader. 1st ed. Thomas Nelson.

6. Blane, Hugh. 2017. 7 Principles of Transformational Leadership: Create a Mindset of Passion, Innovation, and Growth. 1st ed. Weiser.

7. Aldag, Ramon J., and Loren W. Kuzuhara. 2015. Creating High Performance Teams: Applied Strategies and Tools for Managers and Team Members. 1st ed. Routledge.

Chapter Four: Motivation and Ability

Motivation and ability are two critical factors that play a crucial role in an individual's contribution to an organization's goals. An organization can have the best resources, infrastructure, and technology, but its success ultimately depends on the motivation and abilities of its individuals.

In today's fast-paced business world, motivating individuals has become a critical factor for organizations to succeed. Motivation is crucial because it drives individuals to work harder, be more productive, and contribute to the organization's overall goals.

One of the best ways to motivate individuals is by making them feel valued and appreciated. When individuals feel valued and appreciated, they are more likely to be motivated to work harder.

In this chapter, we will explore why employee appreciation is crucial and provide examples of how to motivate individuals.

Why Employee Appreciation is Crucial

Employee appreciation is crucial because it boosts employee morale, increases job satisfaction, and improves employee retention rates. When individuals feel valued and appreciated, they are more likely to feel satisfied with their jobs and work harder to achieve the organization's goals.

This, in turn, leads to increased productivity, better quality of work, and improved job performance. Moreover, when individuals feel valued, they are more likely to stay with the organization, reducing employee turnover rates.

Understanding Motivation

Motivation is one of the most essential aspects of a person's life, as it drives individuals towards achieving their goals and leading a fulfilling life. However, sometimes people may lose their motivation and find themselves struggling to move forward.

In this section, we will explore how to motivate people by assessing their current motivation level, identifying the basic factors that contribute to motivation, evaluating job factors, and considering factors in their private life. We will also provide tips on how to improve motivation and maintain it over time.

The following illustration can be used to better understand factors associated with motivating people:

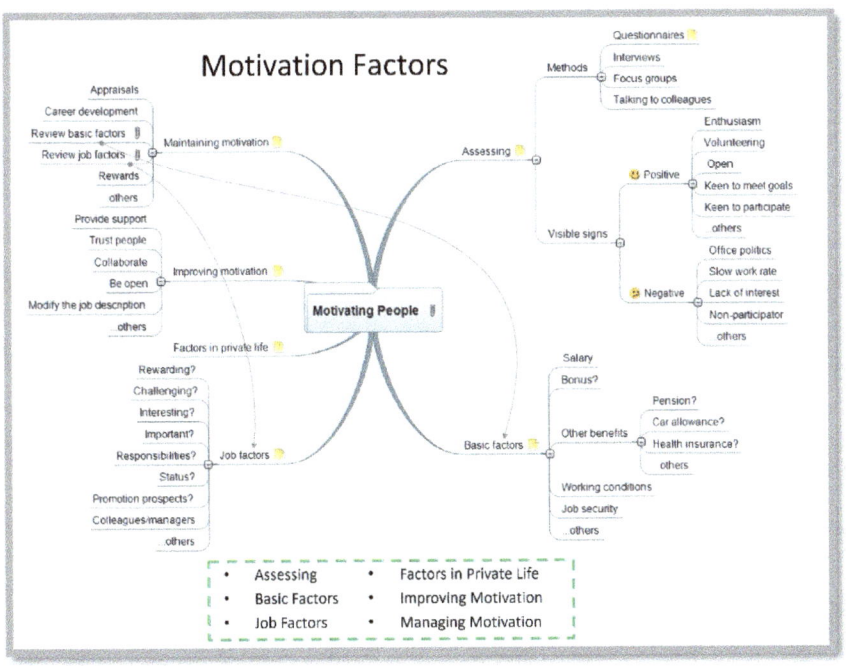

Assessing Motivation Levels

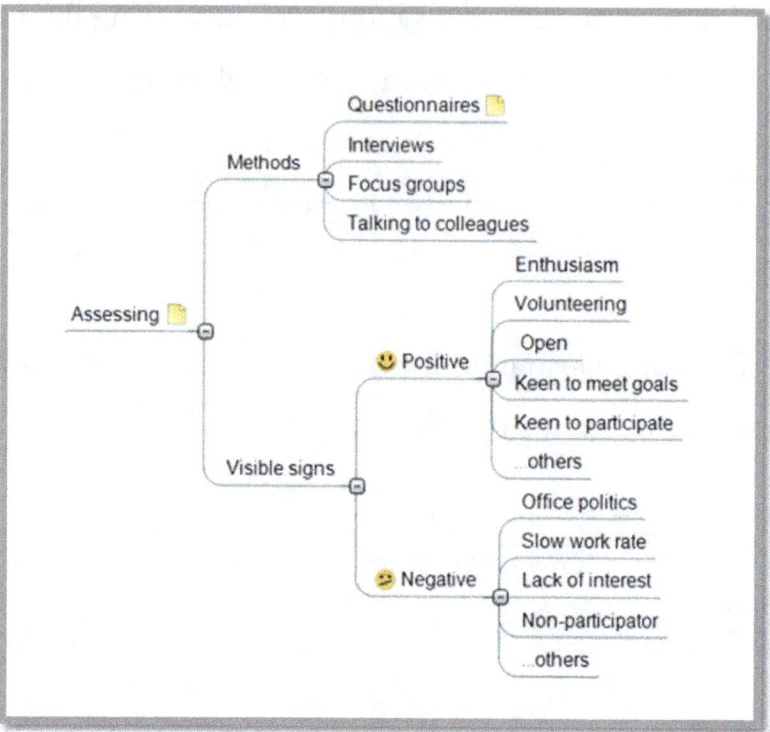

Before motivating someone, it's important to assess their current motivation level. It helps to identify the root cause of their lack of motivation and develop a plan to address it. Some questions to ask include:

- How satisfied are you with your current situation?

- What motivates you?

- What demotivates you?

- What goals do you want to achieve?

Basic Factors Contributing to Motivation

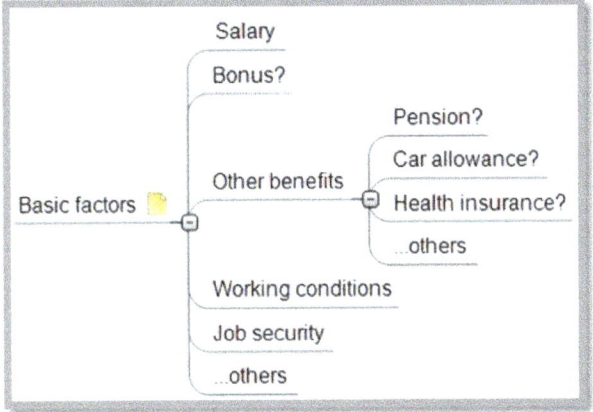

There are some basic factors that contribute to motivation. Some of these factors include:

- Sense of purpose: having a clear sense of purpose and direction in life can motivate individuals to work towards their goals.

- Autonomy: having control over one's work and life can increase motivation as it gives individuals a sense of ownership and responsibility.

- Belief in one's ability to achieve goals: individuals who believe in their ability to achieve their goals tend to be more motivated as they feel confident in their abilities.

Job Factors Contributing to Motivation

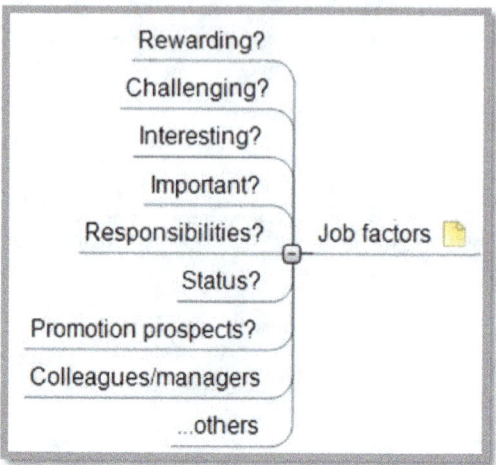

Job factors play a crucial role in motivation. Some of the job factors that can affect motivation include:

- Recognition and rewards: individuals who receive recognition and rewards for their work tend to be more motivated to continue performing well.

- Opportunities for growth and development: having opportunities for growth and development can motivate individuals to continue working towards their goals.

- Supportive work environment: a supportive work environment that promotes collaboration, communication, and a positive culture can increase motivation levels.

Private Life Affecting Motivation

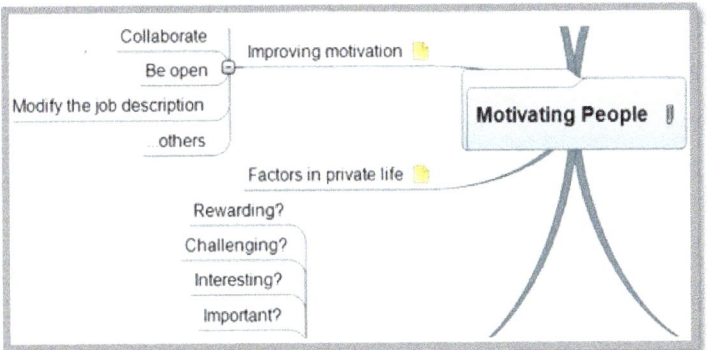

Factors in an individual's private life can also affect their motivation level. Some of these factors include:

- Health and well-being: individuals who prioritize their health and well-being tend to be more motivated as they have the energy and stamina to pursue their goals.

- Relationships: positive relationships with family and friends can provide emotional support and motivate individuals to achieve their goals.

- Hobbies and interests: having hobbies and interests outside of work can provide a sense of fulfillment and motivation to pursue personal passions.

Improving Motivation

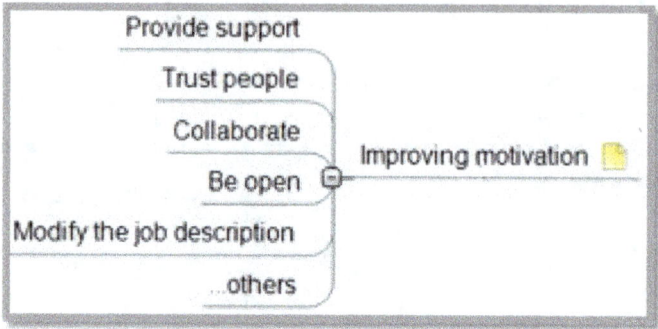

If an individual is lacking in motivation, there are several strategies that can be used to improve motivation levels. These include:

- Setting clear and achievable goals: having clear goals that are achievable can motivate individuals to work towards them.

- Breaking tasks into smaller steps: breaking tasks into smaller steps can make them less overwhelming and increase motivation levels.

- Creating a positive mindset: having a positive mindset and focusing on positive outcomes can increase motivation levels.

Maintaining Motivation

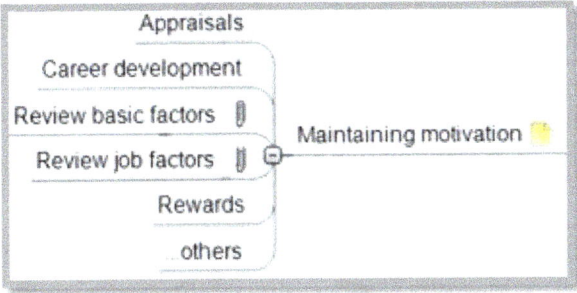

Maintaining motivation over the long term can be challenging, but there are strategies that can be used to help maintain motivation levels. These include:

- Celebrating successes: celebrating successes along the way can provide motivation to continue working towards bigger goals.

- Revisiting goals: revisiting goals and adjusting them as needed can help maintain motivation levels by ensuring they remain achievable and relevant.

- Finally, it is important to remember why we started on our journey in the first place. Reflecting on our initial motivations and the benefits we will gain from achieving our goals can help to rekindle our passion and drive. This can help us to stay motivated and focused on our goals, even during challenging times.

Examples of How to Motivate Individuals

1. Recognition and Rewards

Recognition and rewards are powerful motivators that can help individuals feel appreciated and valued. For instance, you can recognize individuals who go above and beyond their duties by publicly acknowledging their achievements. Additionally, you can offer rewards such as bonuses, paid time off, or gift cards to show your appreciation for their hard work.

2. Opportunities for Growth and Development

Offering opportunities for growth and development is another way to motivate individuals. Individuals who feel they are growing and developing in their careers are more likely to be motivated and engaged in their work. You can offer training programs, workshops, or mentorship programs to help individuals grow and develop their skills.

3. Flexible Scheduling

Flexible scheduling is a powerful motivator that can help individuals balance their work and personal life. Offering flexible scheduling options such as telecommuting or flexible work hours can help individuals feel appreciated and valued. Moreover, flexible scheduling options can improve employee satisfaction and retention rates.

4. Positive Feedback and Constructive Criticism

Positive feedback and constructive criticism are essential to motivate individuals. Offering positive feedback can help individuals feel appreciated and valued. Additionally, constructive criticism can help individuals improve their performance and achieve their goals.

5. Team Building Activities

Team building activities can help individuals feel more connected to their colleagues and the organization. These activities can improve communication, collaboration, and teamwork, leading to increased motivation and job satisfaction. You can organize team building activities such as company outings, charity events, or team-building exercises.

Employee appreciation is crucial to motivate individuals to work harder and contribute to the organization's goals. Recognizing and rewarding individuals, offering opportunities for growth and development, flexible scheduling, positive feedback and constructive criticism, and team building activities are just a few examples of how to motivate individuals. By implementing these strategies, organizations can create a positive work environment where individuals feel valued and appreciated, leading to increased productivity, job satisfaction, and retention rates.

Ability to Perform Tasks

Motivation alone, however, is not enough to achieve success. Individuals also need to have the necessary abilities and skills to perform their tasks effectively. Ability refers to an employee's competence, knowledge, and skills required to perform their job successfully. The ability to communicate, problem-solve, and work collaboratively are just some examples of abilities that individuals may need to possess.

In today's dynamic business environment, organizations need to continuously improve their operations to stay competitive. One of the essential components of this improvement process is ensuring that individuals have the necessary abilities and skills to carry out their duties effectively. This can be achieved by providing training and development programs. These programs help individuals improve their skills and acquire new ones, which not only benefits them but also helps the organization achieve its goals.

When it comes to assessing an individual's ability to perform tasks, there are several factors that can be taken into consideration. As shown in the following illustration, these factors include the individual's experience, personality, education, overall ability to consistently execute, obtaining references on the individual, and testing the individual.

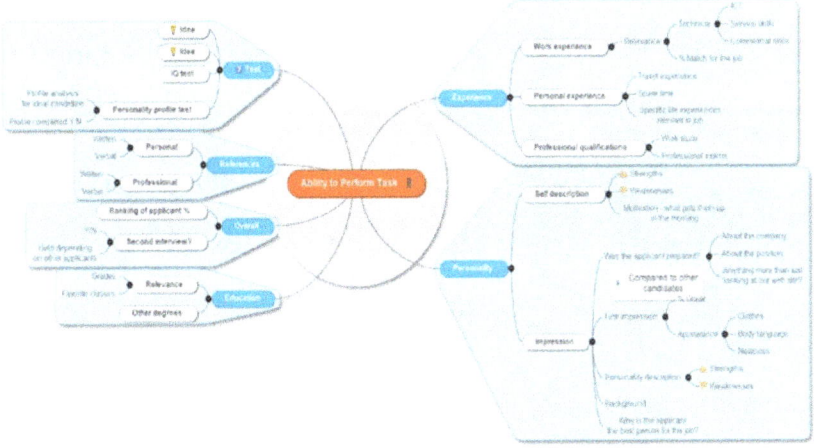

An Individuals Experience

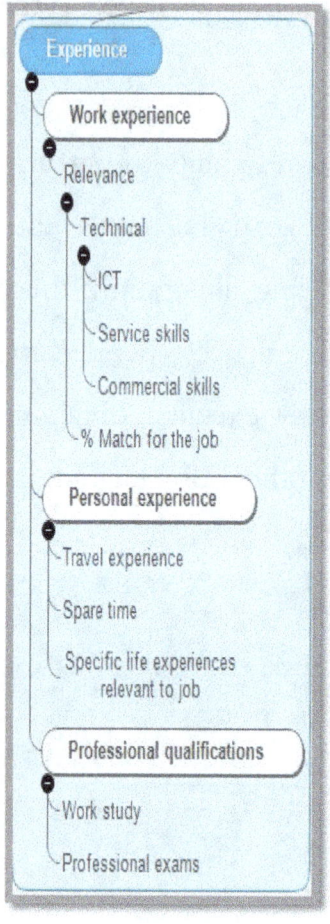

Experience is one of the most important factors when it comes to assessing an individual's ability to perform tasks.

An individual's experience can provide insight into how they have handled similar tasks in the past and may be an indicator of their level of expertise in a future task.

For example, if you are looking for someone to manage a team, you might want to consider someone who has prior experience in a leadership role.

An Individuals Personality

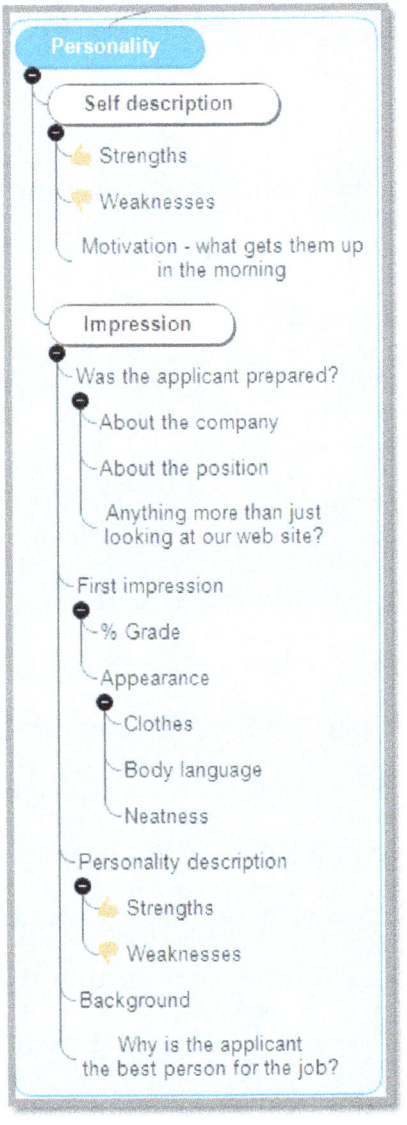

Personality is another factor that can play a role in an individual's ability to perform tasks. Certain personality traits, such as a strong work ethic, resilience, and good communication skills, could make someone more effective in completing tasks.

On the other hand, personality traits like procrastination, lack of attention to detail, or a tendency to avoid confrontation, can hinder an individual's ability to perform tasks effectively.

An Individuals Formal Education

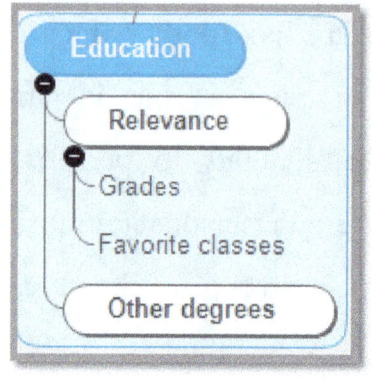

Education can also be an important factor when assessing an individual's ability to perform tasks. Formal education fosters discipline, time management, and a sense of responsibility, which are invaluable traits that contribute to one's overall performance in various tasks.

It provides a foundation of subject-specific expertise, critical thinking abilities, problem-solving techniques, and practical experience, enabling individuals to navigate complex challenges effectively. Whether it's mastering advanced mathematics for engineering, developing language proficiency for effective communication, or acquiring medical knowledge for patient care, formal education cultivates the necessary expertise and prepares individuals to excel in their chosen fields. For example, someone with a degree in engineering may be better equipped to perform technical tasks than someone without that background.

An Individuals Overall Abilities

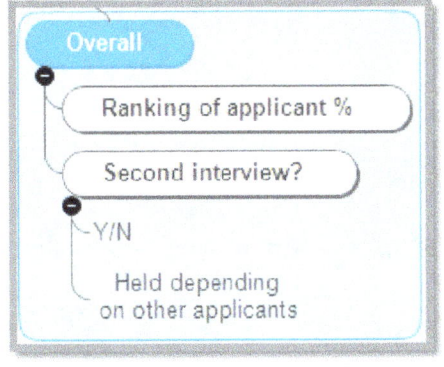

Overall abilities encompass a wide range of general capabilities that greatly influence an individual's success in handling new challenges and adapting to changing circumstances. Problem-solving skills are essential for identifying and addressing complex issues, enabling individuals to analyze situations, explore different options, and find effective solutions.

Critical thinking skills empower individuals to evaluate information, make sound judgments, and approach problems from multiple perspectives, enhancing their decision-making abilities. Attention to detail ensures accuracy and precision in tasks, reducing errors and ensuring high-quality outcomes. These abilities collectively shape an individual's capacity to navigate unfamiliar situations, overcome obstacles, and seize opportunities.

Obtaining References on the Individual

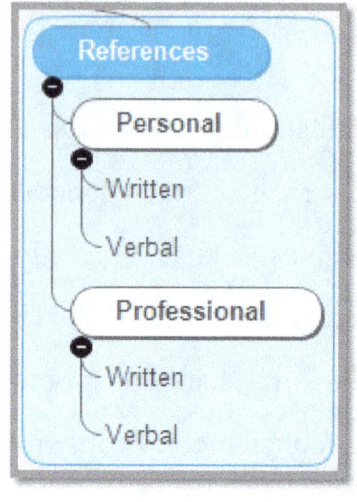

Obtaining references serves as a valuable means to evaluate an individual's ability to perform tasks. When seeking references, engaging in conversations with former employers, colleagues, or professional contacts can offer valuable insights into the individual's work history and performance.

These firsthand accounts shed light on the individual's strengths and weaknesses, providing a comprehensive understanding of their skills and capabilities. References can provide specific examples of the individual's past accomplishments, highlighting their achievements and contributions in similar roles. Additionally, references can reveal valuable information about the individual's work ethic, reliability, and interpersonal skills, which are crucial factors in their ability to perform tasks effectively.

Testing the Individual

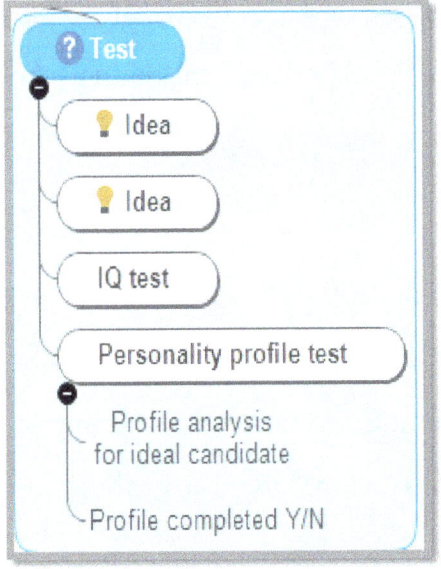

Finally, testing the individual can be a useful way to assess their ability to perform tasks. This may involve anything from skills-based tests to more general assessments of problem-solving abilities or cognitive skills.

There are several factors that can be taken into consideration when assessing an individual's ability to perform tasks. Experience, personality, education, overall abilities, obtaining references on the individual, and testing the individual can all provide valuable insights into an individual's strengths and weaknesses when it comes to performing tasks.

By taking all these factors into consideration, employers can make more informed decisions when it comes to hiring and managing their workforce.

Training and Development Programs

Training and development programs are essential to an organization's success because they enable individuals to acquire new skills and knowledge that can be applied in their jobs.

For example, if an organization adopts new technology, individuals need to learn how to use it effectively. Training and development programs can provide the necessary training to ensure that individuals are proficient in using the new technology.

Similarly, if an organization wants to introduce a new product or service, individuals need to be trained on the product or service's features and benefits.

Organizations can provide training and development programs in various ways, including on-the-job training, off-site training, workshops, seminars, and e-learning programs. On-the-job training involves coaching and mentoring by experienced individuals or supervisors. Off-site training involves sending individuals to external training courses or workshops.

Workshops and seminars are organized by the organization to provide training to its individuals. E-learning programs are online courses that individuals can complete at their own pace.

Training and development programs have several benefits for both individuals and organizations. Individuals who participate in training and development programs have improved job performance, increased job satisfaction, and better career prospects.

Individuals also have higher levels of motivation and engagement, which leads to improved productivity and reduced turnover rates. By investing in their individuals' development, organizations create a positive work environment that fosters loyalty and commitment.

Furthermore, training and development programs help organizations achieve their goals by improving employee skills and knowledge. This can lead to improved customer satisfaction, increased sales, and higher profits. For example, if an organization provides training to its sales team, they will be better equipped to sell the organization's products or services effectively.

This can lead to increased sales and revenue. Similarly, if an organization provides training to its customer service team, they will be better equipped to handle customer complaints effectively, leading to improved customer satisfaction.

Training and development programs are essential to an organization's success. They help individuals improve their skills and acquire new ones, which not only benefits them but also helps the organization achieve its goals.

By investing in their individuals' development, organizations create a positive work environment that fosters loyalty and commitment. Therefore, organizations should prioritize providing training and development programs to their individuals to ensure that they remain competitive in today's dynamic business environment.

Chapter Summary/Key Takeaways

In conclusion, the relationship between motivation and ability is symbiotic. Motivation without the necessary abilities can result in wasted effort and frustration, while ability without motivation can lead to mediocre performance. Therefore, organizations need to ensure that both factors are present and nurtured in their individuals.

Motivation and ability are also interlinked with employee engagement. Engaged individuals are those who are both motivated and have the necessary abilities to perform their job effectively. Such individuals are committed to their work and are willing to go the extra mile to achieve organizational goals.

"Organizations that have a high level of employee engagement often have better performance and are more successful. Engaged individuals not only contribute to the organization's goals but also act as brand ambassadors, attracting and retaining customers and talent."

Motivation and ability are two essential factors that play a critical role in an individual's contribution to an organization's goals. Motivated individuals with the necessary abilities and skills can help an organization achieve success and improve its performance. Therefore, organizations must prioritize both factors and invest in measures to foster them in their individuals.

Chapter Five: Improving the Future State

Organizations that wish to succeed in the long term must ensure that their Executive Leadership, Senior Leadership, and Individual Contributors are all aligned and working towards a shared vision.

Without alignment, an organization's efforts can become disjointed and uncoordinated, leading to inefficiencies, and missed opportunities.

In this chapter, we will explore how to improve the future state of an organization by starting with Executive Leadership, Senior Leadership, and Individual Contributors getting on the same page.

Getting Executive Leadership on the Same Page (Rubik's Cube Level I)

The first step towards getting an organization aligned is to ensure that its Executive Leadership is on the same page. This means that the top leaders in an organization need to have a shared understanding of the company's vision, mission, and values. They also need to agree on the strategic direction of the organization and how they plan to achieve their goals.

If a leader's goal/goals is/are self-serving, one gets a very prejudiced outcome. A leader's responsibility is to identify the "collective" outcome first. If done correctly, this creates the "greater good" and THE metric that everyone in the organization can contribute. The leader becomes the responsible and accountable individual whom is the "keeper of the metric". Decisions are made with respect to that greater good. Once that "greater good" metric is identified, then the work gets done and successes get heralded, but more importantly it sets the stage for succession planning that can be built upon from leader to leader.[8]

To get Executive Leadership on the same page, it's important to create a forum where they can come together and discuss these issues. This can be in the form of regular meetings, retreats, or offsites. These events provide an opportunity for leaders to share their perspectives, clarify their understanding of the company's vision, and identify areas of disagreement.

Once executive leaders are aligned, they can communicate their vision to the rest of the organization. This will help create a sense of purpose and direction for everyone else and ensure that everyone is working towards the same goals. In visual terms, solving the first layer of the Rubik's Cube.

Getting Senior Leadership on the Same Page (Rubik's Cube Level II)

Once the Executive Leadership is aligned (on the same page), the next step is to get Senior Leadership (your middle managers) on the same page. Senior Leadership is the link between Executive Leadership and the Individual Contributors in an organization. They are responsible for translating the vision and strategy set by Executive Leadership into actionable plans that can be executed by the Individual Contributors.

The critical first step to executing well is creating and maintaining a compelling vision of the future that you want even more than you desire your own short-term comfort, and then aligning your shorter-term goals and plans, with that long-term vision.[9]

To get senior leaders on the same page, it's important to communicate the vision and strategy clearly and provide them with the tools and resources they need to execute the plan. This can include training programs, coaching, and mentoring.

It's also important to ensure that Senior Leadership has a clear understanding of their roles and responsibilities. This will help them to align their actions with the goals of the organization and ensure that they are working towards the same objectives. In visual terms, solving the second layer of the Rubik's Cube.

Getting Individual Contributors on the Same Page (Rubik's Cube Level III)

The final step is to get Individual Contributors on the same page. These are the people who are responsible for executing the plans set by Executive Leadership and Senior Leadership. They need to understand the vision and strategy of the organization and how their work contributes to achieving the company's goals.

To get Individual Contributors on the same page, it's important to provide them with regular communication and feedback. This can include regular team meetings, one-on-one sessions with their manager, and performance reviews.

It's also important to ensure that Individual Contributors have the necessary motivation and ability to perform their jobs effectively. This can be achieved through training programs, on-the-job coaching, and mentoring. In visual terms, solving the third and final layer of the Rubik's Cube.

What's next?

As discussed earlier, applying different leadership styles to the future state of an organization can have a significant impact on its success. Each leadership style has its unique advantages and disadvantages, and the choice of which style to implement should be based on the organization's goals, culture, and values.

An authoritarian leadership style can be useful in times of crisis or when quick decisions need to be made, but it can also create a lack of motivation and engagement among individuals. In contrast, a democratic leadership style can promote employee empowerment and creativity, but it can also lead to decision-making delays.

A servant leadership style prioritizes the needs of individuals and focuses on their personal and professional growth, leading to increased loyalty and job satisfaction. Similarly, transformational leadership can inspire and motivate individuals to work towards a shared vision, resulting in higher performance and innovation.

On the other hand, laissez-faire leadership may be suitable in organizations where individuals are highly skilled and self-motivated, but it can also result in a lack of direction and accountability.

"Ultimately, the most effective leadership style depends on the specific context and goals of the organization. Leaders must be flexible and adaptable to change their style to fit different situations and support their teams' growth and success."

The Rubik's Cube has been a popular puzzle toy for decades. It requires a combination of logic, patience, and strategy to solve. Many people believe that the cube can teach valuable lessons about leadership and problem-solving.

In the next section, we will explore "algorithmic thinking" and how known Rubik's Cube algorithms can be used to represent existing leadership "Best Business Practices" and how these practices can be replicated in other business units as future state process improvement initiatives.

Algorithmic Thinking in Leadership

The Rubik's Cube is all about algorithms - a set of instructions that, when followed in the correct order, can solve a problem. Similarly, in the business world, leaders need to think algorithmically to find solutions to complex problems. They need to break down problems into smaller, more manageable parts and identify a series of steps to address each part.

One example of algorithmic thinking in leadership is the "SMART" goal-setting framework. Leaders who use this framework break down a large goal into smaller, more specific objectives that are measurable, achievable, relevant, and time bound.

This approach helps them focus on the most important parts of the goal and measure their progress towards achieving it.

Another example is the "PDCA" cycle (Plan, Do, Check, Act), which is a problem-solving approach used by many companies. This approach involves breaking down a problem into smaller parts, planning a solution, implementing the plan, checking the results, and adjusting the plan if necessary.

Using Rubik's Cube Algorithms to Represent Leadership Best Business Practices

Rubik's Cube algorithms can be used to represent various best business practices in leadership. For instance, the "Cross" algorithm used to solve the first layer of the Rubik's Cube can represent the importance of setting a strong foundation in business operations.

In leadership, this translates to ensuring that the fundamental aspects of a business, such as its culture, vision, and goals, are well-established and communicated to the team.

Another algorithm, the "F2L" (First Two Layers) algorithm used to solve the second layer of the Rubik's Cube, can represent the importance of collaboration and teamwork in business. Leaders who encourage collaboration and teamwork among their team members can leverage the strengths of each individual to achieve the best possible outcome for the organization.

Similarly, the "OLL" (Orientation of Last Layer) algorithm used to solve the third layer of the Rubik's Cube can represent the importance of strategic thinking in business.

Leaders who can think strategically and plan for the long-term can position their organizations for success in a rapidly changing business landscape.

Replicating Best Business Practices in Other Business Units

Once best business practices have been identified, they can be replicated in other business units as process improvement initiatives. For instance, the hiring process can benefit from the SMART goal-setting framework by breaking down the hiring process into specific objectives, such as identifying the necessary skills and qualifications for a specific role and assessing candidates based on those criteria.

Similarly, the PDCA cycle can be applied to the training process by breaking down the training into smaller, more manageable parts and assessing the effectiveness of the training through feedback and metrics.

Chapter Summary/Key Takeaways

In conclusion, getting an organization aligned and working towards a shared vision is critical for long-term success. By starting with getting Executive Leadership, Senior Leadership, and Individual Contributors on the same page, an organization can ensure that everyone is working towards the same goals and objectives.

This requires clear communication, a shared understanding of the organization's vision and strategy, and providing the necessary tools and resources to execute the plan. By following these steps, an organization can create a culture of alignment, teamwork, and success.

The Rubik's Cube can provide valuable lessons about leadership and problem-solving in the business world. By using Rubik's Cube algorithms to represent leadership best business practices, leaders can identify specific steps to address complex problems.

Additionally, by replicating best business practices in other business units as process improvement initiatives, organizations can improve their overall efficiency and effectiveness.

Endnotes

8. Massenburg, Walter, B. USN Vice Admiral (Retired), Email to author, 3 July 2023

9. Moran, Brian P., and Michael Lennington. 2013. The 12 Week Year: Get More Done in 12 Weeks than Others Do in 12 Months. 1st ed. New Jersey: John Wiley & Sons, Inc.

Epilogue/Conclusion

This book aims to explain the importance of leadership alignment and how it can be achieved using the visual analogy of solving a scrambled Rubik's cube, covering multiple topics related to strategic alignment, the need for goals and for individual development with a focus on strategic alignment using a top-down approach.

The different layers of the Rubik's cube represented different layers of responsibilities and accountability within the organization. This book also provides and emphasizes the need for clear-defined leadership alignment goals, and for individuals to understand how their work contributes to achieving these goals.

Additionally, this book highlights the importance of teamwork, employee engagement, and the symbiotic relationship between motivation and ability. Overall, the book provides practical advice on how to create a strong and effective team capable of achieving organizational goals.

The key to leadership is properly diagnosing the development level of individuals, providing autonomy where necessary and support for tasks beyond their current skill level.

Effective teamwork is also essential for achieving success, requiring coordination, collaboration, and a shared vision. Motivation and ability are interlinked with employee engagement, which is crucial for committed and high-performing individuals who are willing to go the extra mile to achieve organizational goals.

Acknowledgments

I would like to express my deepest gratitude to the incredible individuals who have supported and inspired me throughout the process of writing and publishing this book.

First and foremost, I want to thank my loving wife, Leslie. Your unwavering belief in me and your constant encouragement have been the driving force behind my pursuit of this endeavor. Your love, patience, and understanding have been my foundation, allowing me to dedicate countless hours to bringing these words to life. Thank you for always standing by my side.

To my sons, Nicholas and Matthew, you have been my constant source of joy and inspiration. Your presence and infectious enthusiasm have brought light to my life. Thank you for being my motivation and for reminding me of the importance of balance and family in my leadership journey.

I am deeply indebted to my esteemed business mentors and associates, Michael L. George Sr., Michael L. George Jr., and Vice Admiral Walter B. Massenburg, USN (Retired). Your guidance, wisdom, and wealth of experience have shaped me into the leader I am today. Your belief in my potential and your invaluable insights have been instrumental in my growth. I am privileged to have learned from your expertise and to call you not only mentors but also friends.

Finally, I would like to thank the readers who have embraced this book. Your feedback, encouragement, and enthusiasm have been the ultimate reward. Your willingness to explore these pages and engage with the ideas presented within is deeply appreciated.

To all those who have played a role in bringing this book to life, whether through their guidance, support, or belief in my abilities, I am eternally grateful. Your influence has shaped not only this work but also my own personal and professional journey.

With sincere appreciation,

David J. Theilacker

About the Author

Served in the U.S. Navy. Certified Aircraft Pilot. Bachelor of Science degree in Aviation Management, a Master of Aeronautical Science degree and has completed a doctorial internship and numerous doctorial courses in Applied Management and Decision Sciences.

Graduated from the Naval Air Systems Command Senior Executive Management Development Program and served as a Program Manager for Maritime Patrol and Reconnaissance aircraft and Un-Manned Air Vehicles. Certified as a Lean Six Sigma Master Black Belt (MBB).

Received a letter from the White House (signed by the President) and a Meritorious Unit Citation (MUC) from the Director of National Intelligence (DNI) as a process expert.

Owner of a Service-Disabled Veteran Owned Small Business (SDVOSB) and humbled to be a Boat Captain for The Paralyzed Veterans of America (PVA) Bass Tour.